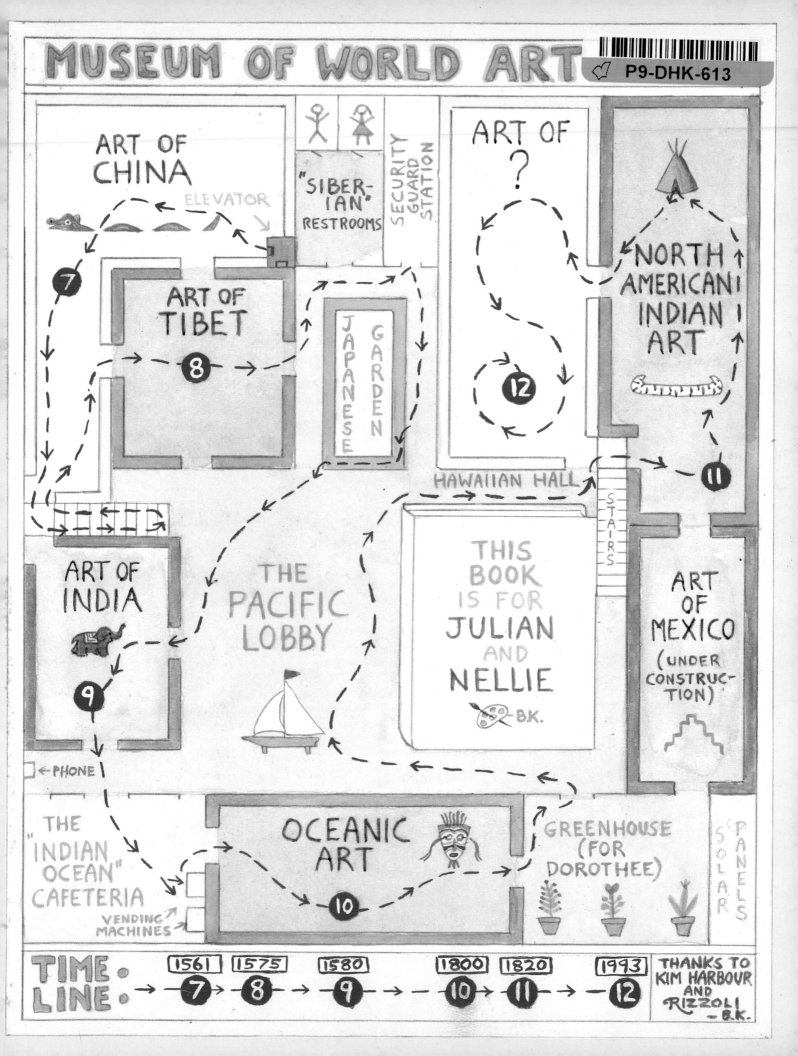

THE GREAT ART
ADVENTURE

THE GREAT ART ADVENTURE

by Bob Knox

RIZZOLI
NEW YORK

Egyptian Wall Painting
Ipuy and His Wife Receiving
Offerings from Their Children
Nineteenth Dynasty
Tomb of Ipuy, Thebes
c.1275 B.C.

This tomb painting shows the Egyptian ideal of representing the human figure: The head is in profile, but the eyes are pictured from the front—as are the shoulders—while the waist and hips are seen in a three-quarters view, and both feet usually show their insteps. Egyptians depicted animals, inanimate objects, and servants in true profiles, however.

Black-Figured Greek Vase
Footrace
Attributed to the Euphiletos Painter
Greece
c. 530 B.C.

Vases such as this featured designs in black silhouetted against the reddish clay of the pottery. The artists scratched in the details with a needle and sometimes added white for accent. Artists later switched to Red-Figured vase design, where the reddish clay designs were featured against black, creating the opposite effect of a Black-Figured vase.

Roman Mosaic
Head of Autumn
Late Classical Period
Roman Empire
Third Century A.D.

Mosaics were made by setting small fragments of colored glass and ceramic tiles into cement or plaster to make pictures. This late classical Roman mosaic represents the god Autumn from the pre-Christian worship of the seasons. After the fall of the Roman Empire mosaics persisted as a motif of Byzantine art, but they featured Christian subjects.

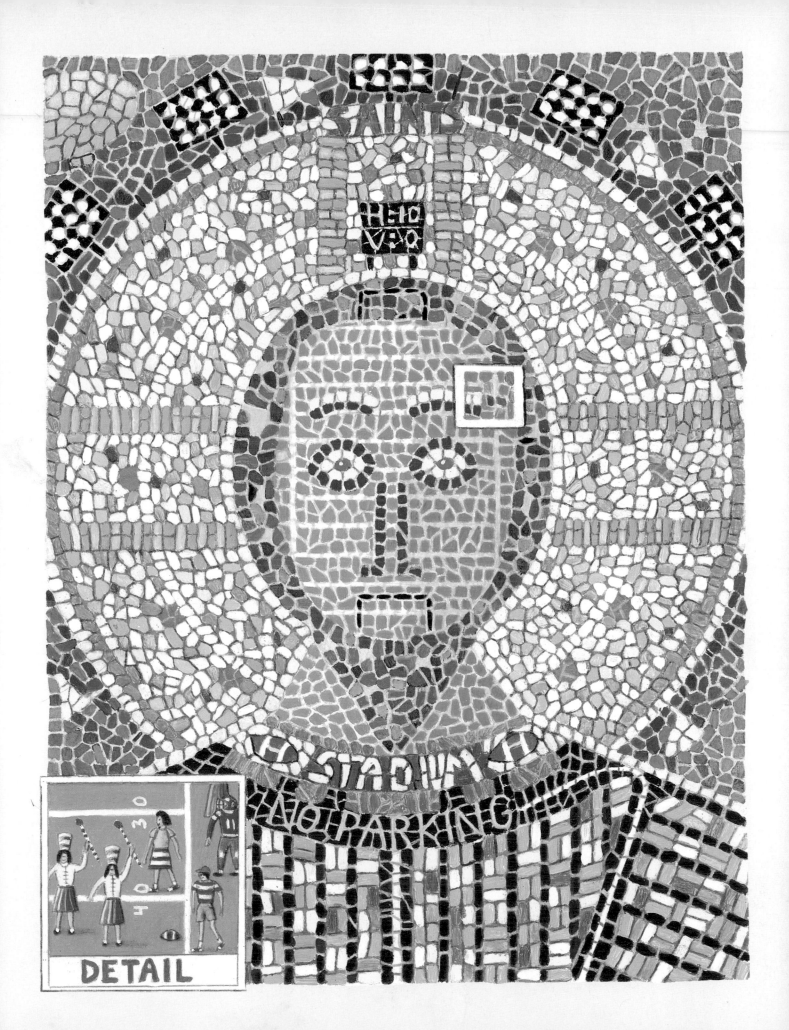

Celtic Manuscript Art
The Book of Kells
The Virgin and Child with Angels
Dublin, Ireland
Early Ninth Century

St. Columba, an early Christian missionary,
started a monastery in Kells around A.D. 806.
The Book of Kells, volumes II and IV, is the
Gospels of St. Mark and St. John, which the
monks of the monastery illuminated (illustrated).
Celtic art featured interlaced and knotted
patterns that expressed a belief in numerology,
the sacred power of numbers.

French Illuminated Manuscript
Très Riches Heures du Duc de Berry
August
By the Limbourg Brothers
Chantilly, France
1413-1416

The wealthy Duke of Berry commissioned three brothers, Paul, Herman, and Jean Limbourg, to illustrate a number of prayer books. *The Book of Hours* was the most elaborate, featuring calendar paintings of typical activities in the Duke's realm during each month. Zodiac symbols referring to the positions of the sun, moon, and planets are shown at the top.

Russian Icon
Bishop Alexey, Metropolitan of Moscow with Scenes from His Life
By Dionisy
Moscow, Russia
1470s

When Grand Prince Vladimir of Kiev married the Byzantine Princess Anna, he agreed to bring Christianity to Russia. This led to the birth of the Russian Orthodox Church and, eventually, to the tradition of sacred icon painting. Around the border of the icon are scenes from the bishop/saint's daily life, which are offered for contemplation.

Chinese Landscape Painting
River Landscape with Towering Mountains (Detail)
By Wen Boren (1502-75)
Ming Dynasty
China
1561

During China's Ming Dynasty (1368 to 1644) painting was done as a hobby, not as a profession, by artists who were well educated and worked for the bureaucracy or were retired. Wu School artists, such as Wen Boren, were noted for the fine, detailed brushwork, subtle use of color, and narrow, vertical formats of their paintings.

Tibetan Scroll
The Indian Pandit Gayadhara
Guru of the Sakya Order
Tibet, Central Regions
Late Sixteenth Century

Tibetan art is Buddhist art, usually depicting deities within their settings. The Sakya Monastery was founded in 1073. This pandit, or master, makes a gesture meaning "teaching" with his right hand. He holds scriptures in his left hand; meanwhile, images of forty-two deities surround him, each of which has a halo and is identified with a label in Tibetan.

Indian Painting
Mughal Period of Akbar
India
Sixteenth Century

We read Western text from left to right, top to bottom; but, in Indian art both the text and the painting are read from right to left. The viewer's eye should enter this painting with the men and the horse at the lower right in prelude to the main scene of the Shah rendering justice to the widow whose son was accidentally killed by someone of his retinue.

MUSEUM
CAFETERIA
(NO TAKE-OUTS)

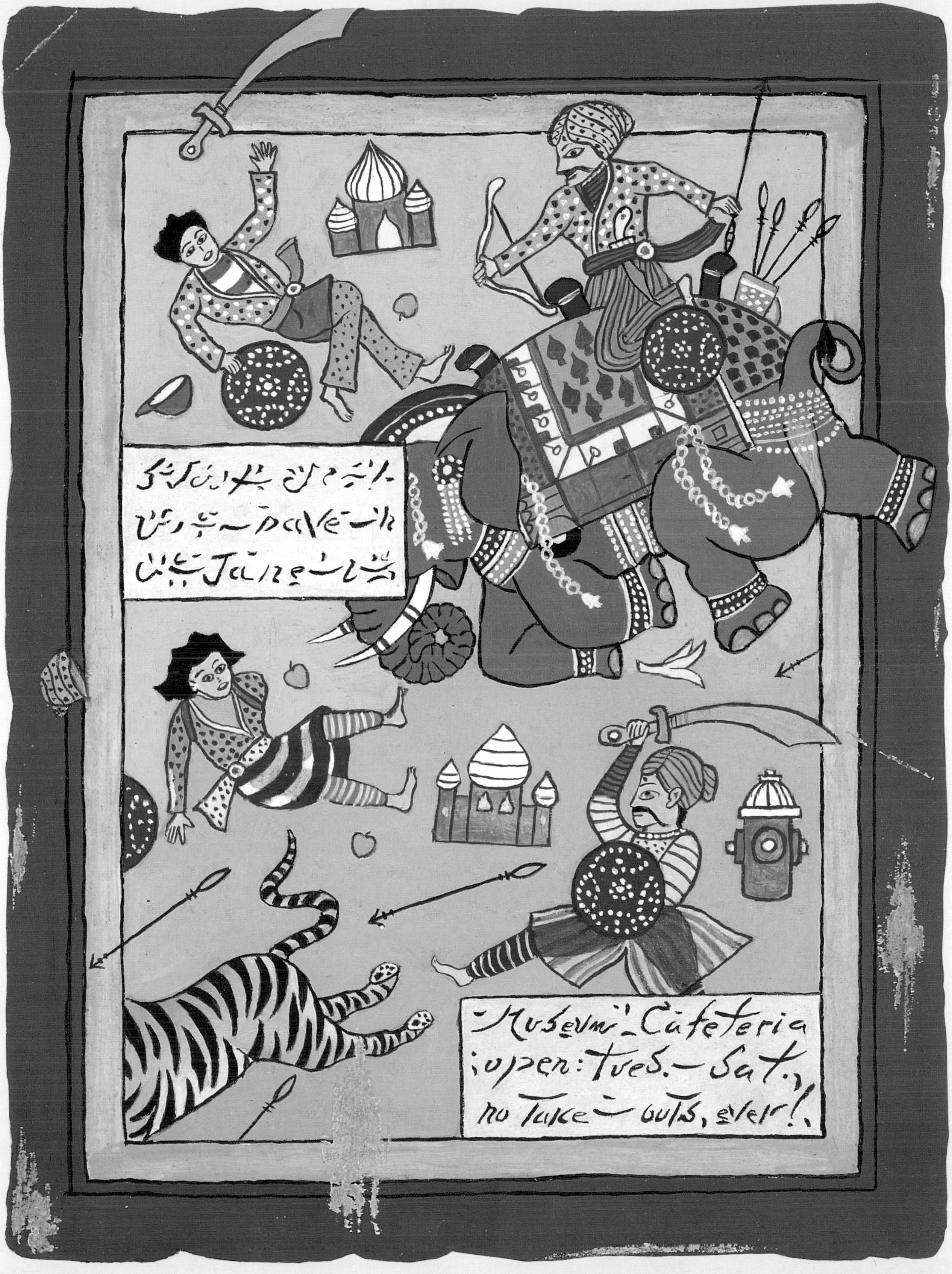
Dave
Jane
Museum Cafeteria
open: Tues.–Sat.,
no take-outs, ever!

Bark Mask
Elema Tribe
Papua, New Guinea
Oceanic-Melanesia
Nineteenth Century

Each family clan in Papua, New Guinea, believed it had a special relationship to specific supernatural beings; therefore, only the members of that clan had the right to represent these beings on masks. Clan elders supervised the work, since they knew the full significance of the geometric symbols. Masks like this one were worn during initiation rites.

Painted Buffalo Robe
Mandan Tribe
North Dakota, U.S.A.
Early Nineteenth Century

For thousands of years North American Indians painted visions, time counts, and personal exploits on animal skins. Explorers Meriwether Lewis and William Clark purchased this painted robe in 1805. Created by a Mandan warrior, its images tell of a battle fought against the Sioux and Arikara Indians around 1797. It is seventy-four inches long.

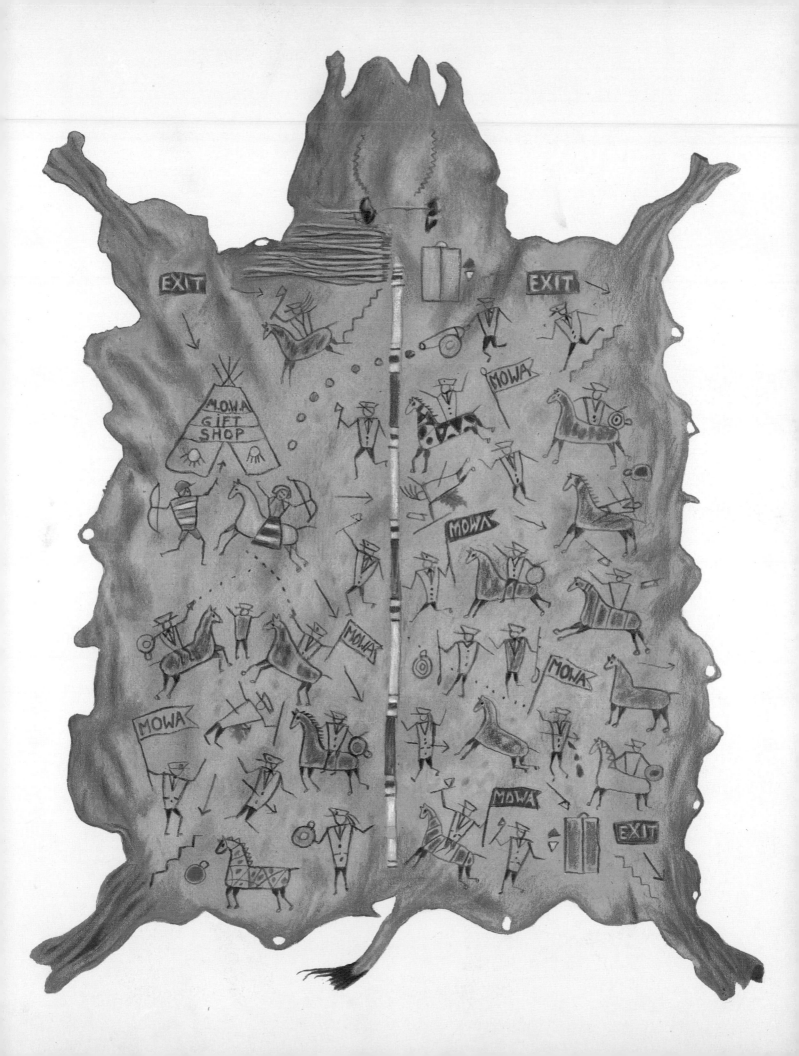

First published in the United States of America in 1993 by
RIZZOLI INTERNATIONAL PUBLICATIONS, INC.
300 Park Avenue South, New York, New York 10010

Illustrations copyright © 1993 by Bob Knox
Compilation © 1993 by Rizzoli International Publications

Library of Congress Cataloging-in-Publication Data

Knox, Bob.
    The great art adventure / by Bob Knox.
        p.   cm.
    Summary: Two children visit the wacky Museum of
World Art, where painting come to life, and they see
such works as Egyptian paintings, Roman mosaics,
Tibetan scrolls, and American Indian buffalo skin
paintings.
    ISBN 0-8478-1688-5
    1. Art—Juvenile literature.   [1. Art—History.
2. Art appreciation.]   I. Title.
N7440.K56   1993
701'.1—dc20   93-20457
                                                  CIP
                                                  AC

Designed by Barbara Balch
Edited by Kimberly Harbour

Printed and bound in Italy

BOB KNOX has "wandered aimlessly throughout the
world in search of the perfect painting." From his birthplace,
New York City, Knox's quest took him to study sculpture at
the Ecole des Beaux-Arts, Rennes, France, in 1971.
He returned to Connecticut just long enough to receive his
bachelor's degree in studio art at Wesleyan University;
then he was off again—exploring Europe and North Africa.
Knox hitchhiked through Tunisia, Algeria, Morocco,
Spain, France, England, and Scotland. He worked as a baker
in Scotland, where he met his wife, Dorothee.
They lived in West Germany for five years, but now reside
in Ridgefield, Connecticut, with their son, Julian,
and daughter, Nellie.

Knox is a favorite cover artist for the *New Yorker* magazine,
where his tongue-in-cheek illustrations have appeared
since 1988. He has exhibited in numerous art galleries.
Knox's motto is "A blank piece of paper is a missed opportunity."

GREENLAND

CELTIC REGION

RUSSIA

4

6

NORTH AMERICA

5 EUROPE

3

2

MID-EAST

12 LAST STOP

ADVENTURE BEGINS!

1

AFRICA

ATLANTIC OCEAN

SOUTH AMERICA

Photo credits: *Page 6.* Egyptian Expedition of the Metropolitan Museum of Art, Rogers Fund, 1930, New York; *Page 8.* Metropolitan Museum of Art, Rogers Fund, 1914, New York; *Page 10.* National Archaeological Museum, Madrid, Spain; *Page 12.* The Board of Trinity College, Dublin, Ireland; *Page 14.* Giraudon/Art Resource, New York; *Page 16.* Cathedral of the Dormition in the Kremlin, Moscow, Russia; *Page 18.* photo by Paul Macapia, Seattle Art Museum, Eugene Fuller Memorial Collection, Seattle, Washington; *Page 20.* photo by John Bigelow Taylor, Tibet House, New York; *Page 22.* Metropolitan Museum of Art, Gift of Alexander Smith Cochran, 1913, New York; *Page 24.* The Michael C. Rockefeller Memorial Collection, Metropolitan Museum of Art, Gift of Nelson A. Rockefeller, 1972, New York; *Page 26.* Peabody Museum of Archaeology and Ethnology, Harvard University, Cambridge, Massachusetts.

TIME. LINE.

1275 B.C.	530 B.C.	250 A.D.	820	1415	1475
1	2	3	4	5	6